THE
NICEST
Sky

BOOK THREE
OF THE TRILOGY

Nicholas D'Andrea, Jr.

THE
NICEST
Sky

BOOK THREE
OF THE TRILOGY

Nicholas D'Andrea, Jr.

dark horse studio
Waterbury, Connecticut, U.S.A.

THE NICEST SKY
Book Three of the Trilogy

To order additional copies of this book, contact:
Xlibris
844-714-8691
www.Xlibris.com
Orders@Xlibris.com

ISBN: 978-1-6698-4157-9 (sc)
ISBN: 978-1-6698-4158-6 (hc)
ISBN: 978-1-6698-4156-2 (e)

Print information available on the last page

Rev. date: 08/17/2022

Photo credits:

Charity-Ann J. Baker
Poems 2, 4, 5, 6, 21, 38.2, conclusion page

Chloe Jane Baker
Poem 32

Emily Creighton
Poems 12, 27

Margherita D'Andrea
Poems 1, 3, 7, 8, 9.1, 11, 13, 15, 16, 17, 19, 20, 22, 23, 26, 28,
30, 33, 35, 36, 37, 38.1, introduction page, table of contents

Nicholas D'Andrea, Jr.
Poems 9.2, 25, 29, 31, 34, cover photo

Gabriel Ducey
Poem 18

Sharon A. Hare
Poem 10

Sue Ryan
Poem 14

To my family and friends
for all their love and support

The sky is big,
become lost in it.
Daydreams abound,
so take it slow.
Peace is your reward.

TABLE OF CONTENTS

1. Summer Comes 2

2. Inspiration 3

3. Autumn 4

4. Dreams 5

5. Souls 6

6. Silver 8

7. When 10

8. The Night 11

9. Into the Rain 13

10. Seasons 16

11. The Trees 18

12. Always Faithful 19

13. The Night Sequel 21

14. Sunshine 23

15. Alasdair's Meadow (Gone) 26

16. If Snowmounds Melt 27

17. The Lighthouse 28

18. Mountains and Valleys 30

19. Through Midnight Shading 32

20. Falling Snow 33

21. The Province 35

22. The Swallows 38

23. Knights in the Sky 39

24. My Love 39

25. Sweet Summer 40

26. Matthew's Passion 41

27. Hansel's Dream 43

28. Lost in Heaven 45

29. Solitude...47

30. Big Things 49

31. Waves...50

32. Morning Woods 51

33. The Jewels of Night 53

34. Fondness 55

35. Dangerous Haven 57

36. Sun Now Faded 59

37. The Lost Dove 60

38. Many Roads...62

1. SUMMER COMES

Winter has come and gone
Now spring is fading, too
I see the sun at dawn
Sparkle in morning dew
And awaken emerald lawn
To welcome the summer view

Reflections uplifting
Sweet memories of you
My life's journey shifting
But my heart remains true
To lazy clouds drifting
Across a palette of blue

As June and July show
And of course August, too
I hope that you will know
I'm dreaming still of you
Under soft moonlit glow
And golden sunshine anew

To your heart my love sings
Autumn's waiting in the wings.

2. INSPIRATION

My inspiration
     deep blue eyes and soft smooth skin
         an ear to listen.

3. AUTUMN

Autumn sings its song
    as the breath of the fall breeze
        gently blows the leaves.

4. DREAMS

Dreams of a new life
       longing to be there with you
              Sweet radio tunes.

5. SOULS

Two souls intertwined
    together by destiny
        beautiful foresight.

6. SILVER

The argentine reflection
      Blinds the hearts of those
            Who once loved vinyl.

7. WHEN

When sunshine rains down on me
And seconds pass like years,
When the silence in your eyes
Comes ringing through my ears,

When autumn leaves paint the ground
And feet tread o'er the canvas

When your love caresses my skin
Your words touch me
Your hands speak to me
Your faith moves me

In disbelief
I can't believe this is happening to me

When icy snow blankets the hills
And stars hide in purple midnight skies
Darkness illuminates my bedroom window
With dreams alive behind closed eyes.

8. THE NIGHT

The night is so grand
When the moon looks down on me,
Making sure your hand
Is in mine so tenderly.

Will you still be here
When morning comes to greet me?

The night fades away
But my dreams will linger on
Throughout the next day
After all the stars are gone.

I still smell your hair
Like it's brushing against me.

If the night fails me
And the moon becomes too shy,
I hope that you will be
In my heart so it will not cry.

In my sleep I hear
Your warm voice comforting me.

9. INTO THE RAIN

If you're going out
Into the rain without me,
Wear your suncoat.
See the flowers drink
A vintage delight
From Heaven's winery.
Share their quenched thirst,
No need for an umbrella…
Splash in joy!
Knowing I am thinking of you.

10. SEASONS

Meadows wandering beneath
skies of purple silk,
summer clouds weaving
through time

Fading rose in autumn heath,
benighted dreams made still,
old seasons grieving
new ones to chime

Satin bows on Christmas wreath
and frost on windowsill,
songbirds never leaving
tunes without rhyme

Childhood joys bequeath
memories old to youthful,
winter now believing
spring will come one more time.

11. THE TREES

The trees cast dappled light upon the ground
as the song of summer brings a new sound
to my ears,
all these years
I've waited for such a day

The trees carry through their leaves
the nostalgic breeze of memories
that evoke tears
of yesteryears,
the summers long gone away

The trees are my soul
my day, my night
my shade, my light

The trees, too, will soon begin to weep
as they ready for their winter sleep
golden tears
will be shed and blown away

The trees are my soul
my day, my night
my shade, my light

The trees dream of waking next spring
to a new life the earth will bring,
a life with no fears
of becoming man's wooden wares,
they shall stand tall another day.

12. ALWAYS FAITHFUL

I will always be
Faithful to you,

You will always see
My love is true

For I'll always be
Faithful to you.

Make a wish
Upon a star
Chase your dreams
Find who you are,

Strange we wished
On the same star
And found our dream
Was never far.

As sure as knowing
The night sky
Holds the glowing
North Star,

I will never
Say goodbye
You're forever
In my heart.

13. THE NIGHT SEQUEL

My eyes see a sky of black,
but I truly believe the world is good.

I live in this black sky…
I was, I am, I will be…

The night and I are forever.

14. SUNSHINE

I miss those good times
When sadness comes to mind
A poignant reminder
Of those halcyon days

I am walking through
Grass so beautifully green
I hear what you're saying
Now I know what you mean

Grand and luscious and blue
Until this great sky is seen
One is not really living
So take in all its beauty

With clarity my eyes
Capture muted sunset
My loneliness dies
Those times I won't forget

Something in my drink that night
Seemed to make it feel just right
And though now you're gone
Looking for someone new
No matter where you are
I'll still be thinking of you.

15. ALASDAIR'S MEADOW (GONE)

Gone is the blood from my veins,
The trips with you down country lanes,
And should I begin to ask myself why,
Glories past felt so compelled to die

Gone from my view are the trains,
To catch a glimpse a green eye strains,
I miss your face as the windows pass by,
To hop aboard I don't even try

Gone from your lips are refrains
Once sung sweetly on open plains,
Now buried beneath hills standing high
Soft passionate voices much too shy

Gone from my hands are the stains
Washed away by cool summer rains,
Once a warm embrace, now a tear in my eye
Caressing my cheek as I whisper goodbye

Gone is the blood from my last vein,
The trips with you down memory lane,
And if I were not to ask myself why
My heart would miss you but never die.

16. IF SNOWMOUNDS MELT

Look at me
        I'll greet your stare,
Kiss me once
        And lose your fear.
Let spring come
        If snowmounds melt
Beneath the warmth
        My face has felt.
Should dead earth hide
        Under fallen leaf,
Breathe life into her
        With a sigh of relief.
The seasons long
        To taste your love,
And touch the skin
        I'm dreaming of.

17. THE LIGHTHOUSE

Once a lighthouse standing tall,
Spraying beams over curved shore,
I couldn't believe I'd lost it all
With hot sand thirsting for more.
The lonely beach has now gone dry
Yet my love is still buried inside.

18. MOUNTAINS AND VALLEYS

I love you
    from the mountains high
    to the valleys wide,
I won't sleep
    'til you're by my side

I imagine your kiss
    on my cheeks
    and return the bliss
    upon vast peaks

Like Mother Nature
    you command rivers to flow
    beneath winds of pleasure
    Oh, how they blow

I'll search
    from the mountains steep
    to the valleys deep,
Until I find you
    I won't sleep.

19. THROUGH MIDNIGHT SHADING

The landscape is changing
    before my eyes,
The crimson clouds hanging
    from evening skies
Bring a grand view
    of loneliness fading
Upon meeting you
    after years of waiting,
I'd thought I was facing
    an endless December
Of sadness erasing
    dreams hard to remember,
But your warmth embracing
    my winter freeze
And eagerly replacing
    with summer breeze
Brought my heart racing
    back to green pasture
To find my soul tracing
    horizons of azure
Where you stand waiting
    to let my eyes see
Through midnight shading
    a new life for me.

20. FALLING SNOW

Snow's falling on
the rooftops
and gently covering all it
comes in contact with,
I love this time of year.

Snow's falling on
the treetops
slowly changing the scene
to white from green
because it's that time of year.

As snow blankets the ground
joy, love, and laughter abound,
the season's merriment
is all around…
It's that time of year.

Snow's falling down
upon the town
to clothe the day
in white lingerie,
It's that time of year.

With stars shining bright
over the countryside,
Winter blues are chased away,
Rejoice in another day.

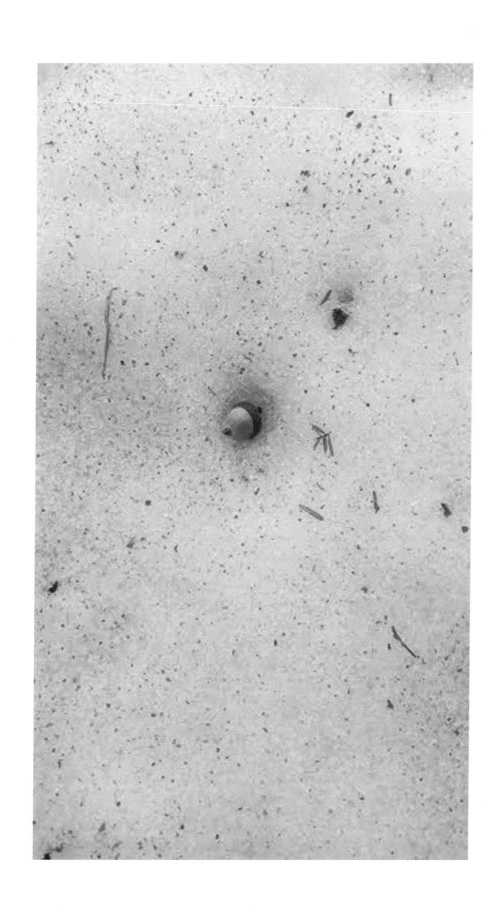

21. THE PROVINCE

He was a boy from the city San Francisco
and moved to a quaint town in the province.

He felt all alone
but could call this place home
where he's lived ever since.

It was here that anger in her voice
forced sweetness in his tears,
waiting for Heaven to take him
from the suffering he'd endured all these years.

But heaven took him
while still on earth
and now he's comforted in your arms,

His head gently rests
upon your warm breasts,
your smile brings
a thousand-and-one charms...

I awoke from my dream
where she takes me back
to a teenage day
when I'm lost in only
happy thoughts,
somewhere by the Bay.

22. THE SWALLOWS

The church bells are ringing
    and swallows are singing
Something's in the air 'round
    San Juan Capistrano.

I smell the fresh scent
    of true romance
Long awaited and warmly welcomed.

Will a swallow come down to me,
Oh, feathered work of art,
Let your wings glide along
    the winding trail
    into my heart.

23. KNIGHTS IN THE SKY

Tiny white soldiers
Marched through the night.
Now standing sentinel
With lustrous armor,
It feels so right.

24. MY LOVE

This is a token
    of my love for you
The words I've spoken
    will always ring true
But my heart's been broken...
    I wish I knew.

25. SWEET SUMMER

Idyllic days beneath summer sun
A life singing dreams come true
I hear lonely angels call me
To join their sweet company
But all I can think of is you.

26. MATTHEW'S PASSION

Matthew's passion
For the rustic cowboy
Ignites royal fireworks
To douse waterworks,
For thirty silver
Sicilienne betrays
With a kiss
The end of days,
Stunning ambiguity
As sun disappears,
Ladies of the night
Quell all fears.

27. HANSEL'S DREAM

Flipping the page
Of scrapbook of old
I came upon her face
In black-and-white photo

Burst into color
So vibrant and clear
Held out my hand
But instead you were there

Sweet sugar cream
Topped with candy delight
A fairy tale come true
In endless night

I feel my dream
Coming to life.

28. LOST IN HEAVEN

I was lost in heaven
The grandest place
Wrapped in satin
And lined with lace
Sewn from only
The happiest dreams
A craft well-done,
Showing no seams.
I felt so warm
Beneath this blanket
A winter storm
Could never freeze it.
I'd start counting sheep
And maybe reach seven
Before falling asleep
And lost in heaven.
So whenever I'm blue
I look to the skies
Of that color, too,
And close my eyes.

29. SOLITUDE

Her pensive eyes
Fall upon a godlike statue.
Relishing the divine daydream,
He returns the silent greeting
With two sapphire gems meeting
A single glance of desire...
One look is not enough
And neither is one touch.

30. BIG THINGS

Lick the postage on the box
Then send it on its way,
Big things surprisingly come
In delicately small packages,
So let this sensual night
Seduce the ravishing day.

31. WAVES

Waves of pleasure
Drift over
A sea of white,
Stars on water
Beneath the night.
Set sail now,
The winds agree
To take us home
In ecstasy.

32. MORNING WOODS

The sun comes up over my head
While I'm still lying in my bed
Trees outside my windows
Cast shadows
Over my body
Their branches strong and firm
While rays shine upon me.

Trees watching over me
from their own winter haven
reach out to guide me along
the cold road of emptiness…
What am I searching for?

I feel smooth skin
warm frostbitten hands,
the sun will begin
to cast white diamonds
across the horizon,
lighting afire
trees adorning the landscape.

Now I feel closer to you
as this dream I hold
fills my soul,
the trees rise this morning
with sunshine a willing partner.

The warmth will melt the ice
and dry my eyes,
you are a new season
of life reborn
with new adventures
keeping tight hold
of old memories.

Morning woods,
Such beautiful trees.

33. THE JEWELS OF NIGHT

I'm mesmerized
    by the jewels of night
As a warm cloak
    of darkness envelops me

How I've waited for life
    to come sailing
    just around the bend

With dreams of love
    closely trailing
    and happiness to never end

You helped me plant
    a garden of memories
    with seeds of grace,

The fragrance here
    will please
    beneath a canopy
    of trees

I want to revisit
    this place,
Hear the upbeat music
    with me.

34. FONDNESS

My summer nights without you
Turn to winters of despair,
Too homesick to see you standing there
Shrouded in a mist of nostalgia,
Take me back to those childhood days…
All that I loved and all that I missed,
All that I wished
Was to know you then
But still have you now.

My world came crashing down…
It was on that day
We walked the grassy path
To the old barn of red
And became married to
A virgin summer love
With heartwarming memories.

My tears are shed with fondness
Of our love.

35. DANGEROUS HAVEN

I must have worn out my welcome
Because this place has just become
Nothing but a dangerous haven -
Ship's left shore, but you're not wavin'

Really came to drop anchor
In your alluring harbor -
Caught off guard by the siren
And pulled into a dangerous haven

Not your run-of-the-mill sailor
Yet my question is dodged by your answer -
I'm really just an innocent lad
Not knowing why you think I'm bad

A storm has blown me off course
I didn't know things could get any worse -
The wind hit my face like a whip
As it tried to destroy my ship

Now I'm the Captain if you haven't guessed
How I'm to achieve the height of success
But abandoned, all my seamen left me -
It was either that or mutiny!

So the sun the night sky does consume
When eyes fail and shadows loom -
With head held low and sails tattered
The waves carry off a heart shattered.

36. SUN NOW FADED

Beneath leafless trees
The winter seems hated
As the green grass flees
No longer shaded

Smiles turn jaded
Are perhaps overstated
The sun has now faded

For so long I've waited
The time's finally come
I feel so elated
My journey now done.

37. THE LOST DOVE

The one I'm thinking of
Is not with me today,
It is my little dove
Who has flown away.
Not just for the winter
It's sad for me to say,
I really do miss her -
Why did she fly away?

38. MANY ROADS

There are many roads
in life
Will you pick one…
or travel many?
What are the chances
our paths would cross?
So many roads
and yet ours met…
so glad
they did,
So happy
we met.
I walk off with you
Into the sunset.

Proof that the apple certainly has fallen far from the tree.
But the apple hasn't been bruised. It merely kissed the ground upon impact.
Red, shiny, sweet, juicy, refreshing.
So beautiful it tempts even the most outspoken critic of vegetarianism.
After all, every man needs a little fruit with his meat.